EXTREME LIFE

GOLIATH BIRD-EATING SPIDERS

AND OTHER EXTREME BUGS

BY DEIRDRE A. PRISCHMANN

Consultant:
Gary Dunn
Director of Education
Young Entomologists' Society
Minibeast Zooseum
Lansing, Michigan

Capstone
press®

Mankato, Minnesota

Fact Finders are published by Capstone Press,
151 Good Counsel Drive, P.O. Box 669, Mankato, Minnesota 56002
www.capstonepress.com

Library of Congress Cataloging-in-Publication Data
Prischmann, Deirdre A.
　　Goliath bird-eating spiders and other extreme bugs / by Deirdre A. Prischmann.
　　p. cm. — (Fact finders. Extreme life)
　　Summary: "Describes the world of arthropods, including characteristics, life cycles, and
defenses" — Provided by publisher.
　　Includes bibliographical references and index.
　　ISBN–13: 978–1–4296–1267–8 (hardcover)
　　ISBN–10: 1–4296–1267–3 (hardcover)
　　1. Tarantulas — Juvenile literature. 2. Arthropoda — Juvenile literature. I. Title. II. Series.
QL458.42.T5P75 2008
595.7 — dc22　　　　　　　　　　　　　　　　　　　　　　　　　　　2007026965

Editorial Credits
Megan Schoeneberger and Lori Shores, editors; Alison Thiele, designer and illustrator;
　　Linda Clavel, photo researcher

Photo Credits
Alex Wild Photography, 9, 24–25
AnimalsAnimals/OSF/John Mitchell, 13
Bruce Coleman Inc./Carol Hughes, 26
Forestry Images/Bugwood.org/Hannes Lemme, 6 (bottom left); Stanislaw Kinelski, 6 (bottom
　　right); Département de la Santé des Forêts, Bugwood.org/Louis-Michel Nageleisen, 6 (top right);
　　Office National des Forêts, Bugwood.org/Daniel Adam, 6 (top left)
Minden Pictures/Konrad Wothe, 15
Natural Visions/Jeremy Thomas, 29
Photo Researchers, Inc/G. Ronald Austing, 18; John Mitchell, cover; Ted Kinsman, 19
Shutterstock/Cathy Keifer, 5; Daniel Gustavsson, 16–17; Dr. Morley Read, 7; John Bell, 20–21; Steve
　　McWilliam, 22–23
Visuals Unlimited/Dr. James L. Castner, 11

1 2 3 4 5 6 13 12 11 10 09 08

TABLE OF CONTENTS

CHAPTER 1

BUGS ARE EVERYWHERE

Can vampire moths suck your blood? Can fishing spiders swim? Yes! These are just a couple of examples of extreme bugs.

Most people call anything that creeps and crawls a bug. True bugs, however, are a specific type of insect. And some scientists believe there are more than 30 million kinds of bugs!

Creepy crawlies are really a group of animals called arthropods. Spiders, scorpions, centipedes, and insects are all arthropods. All these animals have jointed legs, bodies with segments, and a tough, outer covering called an exoskeleton.

thorax: the body part between an insect's head and abdomen

All arthropods have features in common, but each group is different. Insects have only six legs while spiders have eight legs. Insects have three main body parts: the head, **thorax**, and abdomen. Spiders only have two main body parts. A spider's head and thorax are combined and called a cephalothorax.

EGG

LARVA

PUPA

ADULT

Growing Up Buggy

Caterpillars look like they have more than six legs. Are they still insects? Yes! The six-legged rule means insects must have six legs on their thorax sometime during their **life cycle**. Eggs and caterpillars are butterflies at different stages in their life cycle. Caterpillars may look like fat worms, but they will change into colorful butterflies with six legs.

katydid

metamorphosis: how an insect's body changes during its life cycle

Butterflies and many other insects go through complete **metamorphosis**. They change from eggs to larvae to pupae to adults. Other insects, like grasshoppers and katydids, go though gradual metamorphosis. They change from eggs to nymphs to adults. Nymphs look like adults, but they don't have fully developed wings.

CHAPTER 2

UNUSUAL NEIGHBORHOODS

If you flip over a big rock, you'll likely see a few insects. But arthropods don't just live under rocks. They are found in almost every habitat on the planet. You can find bugs in soil, on plants and animals, and even in manure. Bugs live in freshwater and saltwater lakes, cool caves, and hot deserts. Some fleas even make their home on seals in Antarctica.

Ice Is Nice: Rock Crawlers

People are warm-blooded. Our bodies make heat by burning food. Unlike humans, arthropods are cold-blooded. They depend on their surroundings for warmth.

WEIRD!

Goldenrod gall fly larvae like the cold too. They can stay alive even when ice crystals form inside their bodies!

Most insects can barely move if it's too cold, and they often freeze to death. But rock crawlers are one exception. They like it frosty. In fact, the warmth of your hand can kill a rock crawler! Rock crawlers' bodies can stand temperatures below freezing. They live high in the mountains in caves or near icy glaciers and snowfields. Scientists are still trying to figure out how rock crawlers can survive such extreme cold.

maggot: another name for fly larvae

parasite: a bug that lives on or in another animal

GROSS!

Screwworms often attack the navels of newborn cattle.

Home Sweet-Meat Home

Imagine living inside a gingerbread house. If you were hungry, you could reach out and grab a snack. Screwworm **maggots** do just that. But it is an animal's body that serves as their home and food. These **parasites** feed on blood and use hook-shaped mouthparts to scrape at the warm flesh.

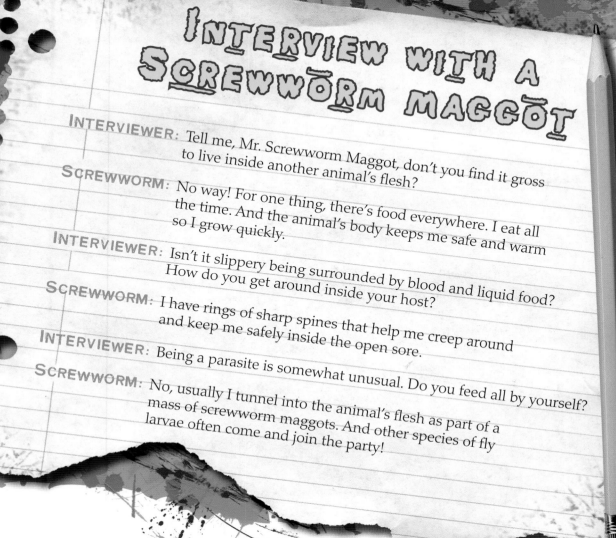

INTERVIEW WITH A SCREWWORM MAGGOT

INTERVIEWER: Tell me, Mr. Screwworm Maggot, don't you find it gross to live inside another animal's flesh?

SCREWWORM: No way! For one thing, there's food everywhere. I eat all the time. And the animal's body keeps me safe and warm so I grow quickly.

INTERVIEWER: Isn't it slippery being surrounded by blood and liquid food? How do you get around inside your host?

SCREWWORM: I have rings of sharp spines that help me creep around and keep me safely inside the open sore.

INTERVIEWER: Being a parasite is somewhat unusual. Do you feed all by yourself?

SCREWWORM: No, usually I tunnel into the animal's flesh as part of a mass of screwworm maggots. And other species of fly larvae often come and join the party!

Female screwworm flies can lay up to 300 eggs near wounds or openings, such as nostrils. Within a day, maggots hatch from the eggs and start eating. Screwworms can tunnel nearly 6 inches (15 centimeters) into an animal's body, which is farther than seven pennies in a row!

CHAPTER 3

GETTING GRUB

Super-Sized Spiders

When you see a spider in your home, often it's the size of a gumball. In tropical rain forests, many spiders are larger than baseballs. The goliath bird-eating spider is as big as a basketball when its legs are spread out.

Being a super-sized spider has advantages. The goliath bird-eating spider has large fangs and deadly **venom**. This big tarantula can attack larger animals like frogs and bats. But even though goliath spiders are huge, they are quiet hunters. They sneak up and pounce on their prey. They can even climb trees and catch birds. That's quite a meal for a spider!

venom: a poisonous liquid made by some animals

CRAZY!

When a goliath bird-eater feels threatened, it can make a very loud hissing noise by rubbing bristles on its legs together!

Look away from the Light

Some insects don't waste energy hunting. Instead, they let their food come to them. Some crafty bugs catch their prey in homemade traps.

Australian glowworms are a kind of fungus gnat larvae, or maggot. As their name suggests, they glow in the dark. They live in moist, dark caves in Australia and New Zealand.

These glowworms have a clever way of catching food. First they spin webs of long sticky threads that hang down from the cave ceiling. Then they do what comes naturally — they glow! Flying insects are attracted by the glowworms' light. But when bugs fly too close, they get caught in the sticky threads. Voila! Dinner is served!

GROSS!

The sticky droplets on the glowworm's web have chemicals that stop the prey from fighting as it is eaten.

Super Spider Soup

SERVING SIZE: Enough for one goliath bird-eating spider

INGREDIENTS: One bird, frog, or bat, venom, and digestive chemicals

STEPS:

1. Capture your choice of meat.
2. Bite animal and release venom into its body.
3. When victim stops moving, spit chemicals into its body to turn the meat into liquid.
4. Slurp up and enjoy!

CHAPTER 4

DON'T EAT ME!

Would you eat a grasshopper? Does the thought of live insects wriggling around in your mouth make you squirm? It might not sound good to you, but lots of animals eat bugs. Predators like birds, bats, and amphibians gobble up thousands of bugs every day. So how do insects avoid being dinner?

Invisible Insects

Some insects are masters of disguise. They trick their enemies into thinking they aren't insects at all. Walking sticks look like twigs. They are mostly green or brown and are long and thin. Leaf insects have flattened legs and bodies that look like leaves. They are greenish and often have sharp spines. Many adults flick their eggs to the ground. The eggs are hard to see because they look like seeds.

WEIRD!

Plant-eating leaf insects from Southeast Asia look and act so much like leaves that they sometimes try to eat each other!

Looking like plants is not the only way these bugs pretend to be sticks and leaves. Stick insects often stretch out their front legs and freeze, like a nonmoving twig. When the wind blows, stick and leaf insects sway along with the rest of the tree parts.

If a predator is not fooled, stick insects can defend themselves. The two-striped walking stick sprays smelly chemicals from its thorax. The giant prickly stick insect pretends to sting by curling its abdomen like a scorpion.

Tasting Terrible

Other insects move around in daylight and are brightly colored. Why don't they get eaten?

Milkweed bugs feed on seeds of milkweed plants, which have harmful chemicals. These chemicals don't hurt the milkweed bugs. But when predators eat milkweed bugs, the chemicals in the bugs' bodies make them sick. The predators relate the black and orange pattern of milkweed bugs to a bad experience. Advertising can pay off!

CHAPTER 5

FIGHTING BACK

Most arthropods that have warning colors want to be seen by predators. But this type of defense might not protect arthropods if it's dark. So what about insects that move around at night? Some use sound to defend themselves against enemies. Tiger moths make clicking noises when attacked by bats. The noise confuses the bats by disturbing the echoes they listen for to locate prey.

If you've ever been stung by a wasp, you know that insects can defend themselves. But not all insects have stingers. Some insects attack predators with venom and sharp fangs. Others squirt their own blood or vomit on enemies to keep them away. Some arthropods even attack their enemies in large groups. Don't be fooled by their size! Bugs can put up a good fight.

Scolopendra centipedes hold enemies with claw-like legs and poison them with venom.

What's That Noise?

Many people know what roaches look like because these insects often live in houses. But Madagascar hissing cockroaches live on the rain forest floor. They are active at night and hard to see because they're dark colored.

Even so, many animals eat cockroaches, including birds and reptiles. But Madagascar hissing cockroaches have a special defense against predators. These roaches hiss when they are disturbed. They make the sound by forcing air out of breathing holes called **spiracles**. Hissing can surprise a predator and give the cockroach a chance to get away.

spiracles: small breathing holes on an insect's body

WEIRD!

Madagascar hissing cockroaches also hiss when they are mating.

Master Blasters: Nasute Termite Soldiers

Termites are social insects like wasps and bees. They live in underground colonies and work together. Termite soldiers protect their nest from predators like ants.

Some kinds of termite soldiers are called nasutes. They have rounded heads with long, pointy snouts. Nasutes are blind, but they still find their enemies easily using their sense of smell. Once they've located the dangerous intruders, the nasutes attack with fluids they spray from their snouts. The fluids are sticky and tangle up the predator's legs and body. The liquid's odor attracts more nasute soldiers to help spray enemies and defend the colony.

GROSS!

Because nasutes have tiny mouthparts and can't chew, worker termites throw up and feed them the vomited food.

fishing spider

Unbelievable Bugs

Arthropods have been around for at least 300 million years. That's a long time! Although spiders, scorpions, centipedes, and insects are dramatically different from one another, they are all arthropods. Their weird-looking bodies and strange behaviors help them survive. While bugs may look and act odd, these extreme animals are the ultimate survivors.

Five More Super Amazing Arthropods!

1 Some leaf-feeding beetle larvae keep predators away by storing mounds of their own poop on their body. Any predator wanting to eat those larvae would have to accept a mouthful of poop as an appetizer!

2 Fireflies are beetles that make light. They flash their light on and off to find mates. But some females change their flash pattern to trick males of other species. Males fly down to mate, and instead get eaten!

3 Asian vampire moths use sharp, tube-like mouthparts to suck blood from animals, including humans. Other moth species feed on sweat and tears.

4 Bombardier beetles attack enemies by spraying them with hot, bad-tasting liquid.

5 Fishing spiders are found near freshwater and are able to dive and swim. These spiders can even catch frogs.

True Lives of Scientists

Medical Entomologists

Standing in a noisy poultry house, two people collect sticky traps hanging over pits full of stinky poop. They are counting flies. It's all in a day's work for scientists called medical **entomologists**.

Many bugs, like flies, can cause diseases by infecting people and animals with bacteria and viruses. Medical entomologists study arthropods to understand the link between bugs and disease. In tropical areas these scientists often need pills and shots so they don't catch diseases from the bugs they study.

entomologist: a scientist who studies arthropods

GROSS!

Some entomologists study maggots on a body to learn how long a person has been dead.

Entomologists also work in laboratories. They wear lab coats and gloves for protection while they cut open ticks or grind up mosquitoes. No matter what they are doing, medical entomologists are trying to keep us safe from disease.

GLOSSARY

ENTOMOLOGIST (en-tuh-MAH-luh-jist) — a scientist who studies arthropods

LIFE CYCLE (LIFE SYE-kuhl) — the series of changes a living thing goes through from birth to death

MAGGOT (MAG-uht) — fly larva

METAMORPHOSIS (meht-uh-MOR-fuh-siss) — the series of changes some animals go through as they develop from eggs to adults

PARASITE (PAIR-uh-site) — an animal or plant that lives on or inside another animal or plant

PREDATOR (PRED-uh-tur) — an animal that hunts other animals for food

PREY (PRAY) — an animal hunted by another animal for food

SPIRACLE (SPIHR-uh-kul) — openings on an insect's body where it gets air

THORAX (THOR-aks) — the part of an insect's body between the head and the abdomen

VENOM (VEN-uhm) — poisonous liquid produced by some animals

Internet Sites

FactHound offers a safe, fun way to find Internet sites related to this book. All of the sites on FactHound have been researched by our staff.

Here's how:

1. Visit *www.facthound.com*

2. Choose your grade level.

3. Type in this book ID **1429612673** for age-appropriate sites. You may also browse subjects by clicking on letters, or by clicking on pictures and words.

4. Click on the **Fetch It** button.

FactHound will fetch the best sites for you!

Read More

Dell, Pamela. *Do Bed Bugs Bite?: A Book about Insects.* Why in the World? Mankato, Minn.: Capstone Press, 2007

Stewart, Melissa. *Maggots, Grubs, and More: The Secret Lives of Young Insects.* Brookfield, Conn.: Millbrook Press, 2003.

Winner, Cherie. *Everything Bug: What Kids Really Want to Know about Insects and Spiders.* Chanhassen, Minn.: NorthWord Press, 2004.

INDEX